Alpha Book Publisher
www.alphapublisher.com

Ordering Information:
Quantity sales. Special discounts are available on quantity purchases by corporations, associations, and others. For details, contact the publisher at the address above.
For orders by U.S. trade bookstores and wholesalers, visit www.alphapublisher.com/contact-us to learn more.

Printed in the United States of America

# INTRODUCTION

*A Path Between the Sun and Moon* is the third book in my continuing collection of original quotations, poems, and other short-form writings. These writings evolved from eight years spent primarily in silence, immersed in the natural order. They were channeled by the Higher Source of wisdom which inhabits each of us—if we are but quiet enough to listen.

Time and experience have shown me that silence is a spiritual gift of inestimable value, one whose wisdom is increasingly lost in the turbulent, digital world in which we live. My greatest desire is that something that came from the silence within me, will somehow connect to and inspire the wisdom within you.


Blair F. Borders
West Palm Beach, FL
Sept. 17, 2022

# ACKNOWLEDGEMENTS

I'd like to thank my mother, Rosalind Borders, for her unconditional love and lifelong encouragement of my creative endeavors.

Original photography by Rosalind Borders and Blair F. Borders.
Additional photography - Internet Public Domain

# A Path Between
# the
# Sun and Moon

To walk alone through life, is to be wounded by the moon and forsaken by the sun—a child of light lost in shadow.

# A Path Between the Sun and Moon

Before blossoming
into this world,
many of life's most
precious gifts
germinate in silence.

# A Path Between the Sun and Moon

Those who become lost in the physical fail to appreciate the metaphysical, and every beautiful dimension in between.

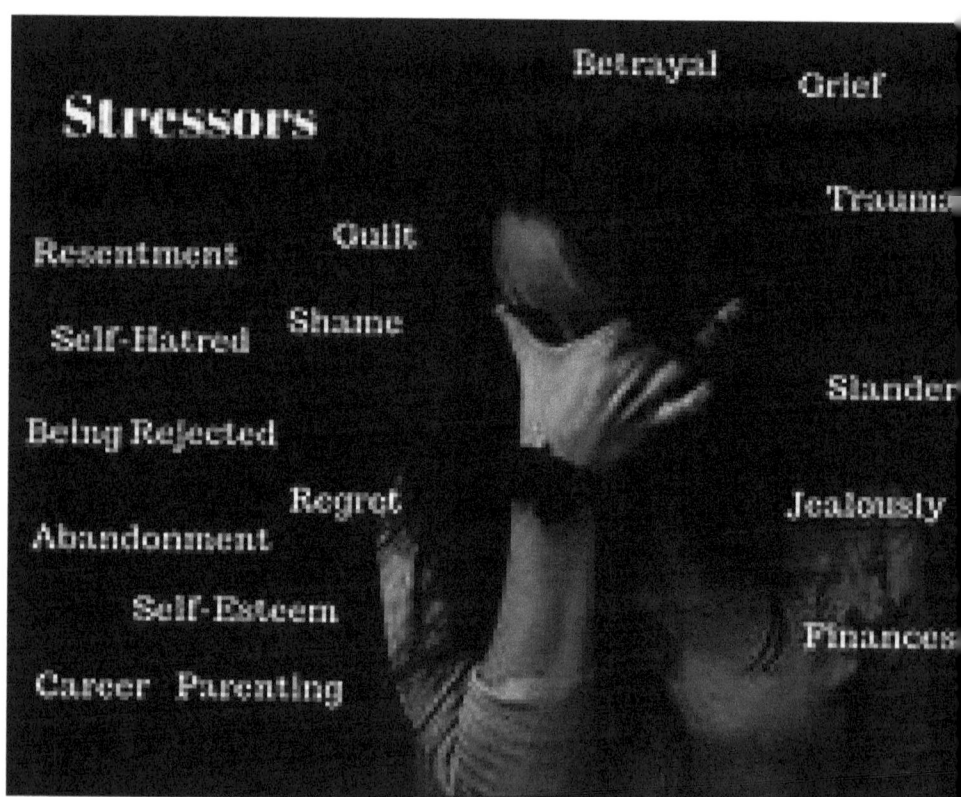

The mind, riddled
with toxic emotions,
becomes the source
of untold misery.

# A Path Between the Sun and Moon

The spiritual life isn't about becoming who you are, it's about unbecoming who you are not.

Some questions shouldn't be answered; others shouldn't be asked.

If your entire life revolves around the belief that "time is money," you'll end up spiritually bankrupt.

# A Path Between the Sun and Moon

All so-called obstacles are potentially surmountable— some physically, externally—and others inwardly, spiritually.

Most people only theoretically appreciate what they haven't temporarily—or permanently—lost.

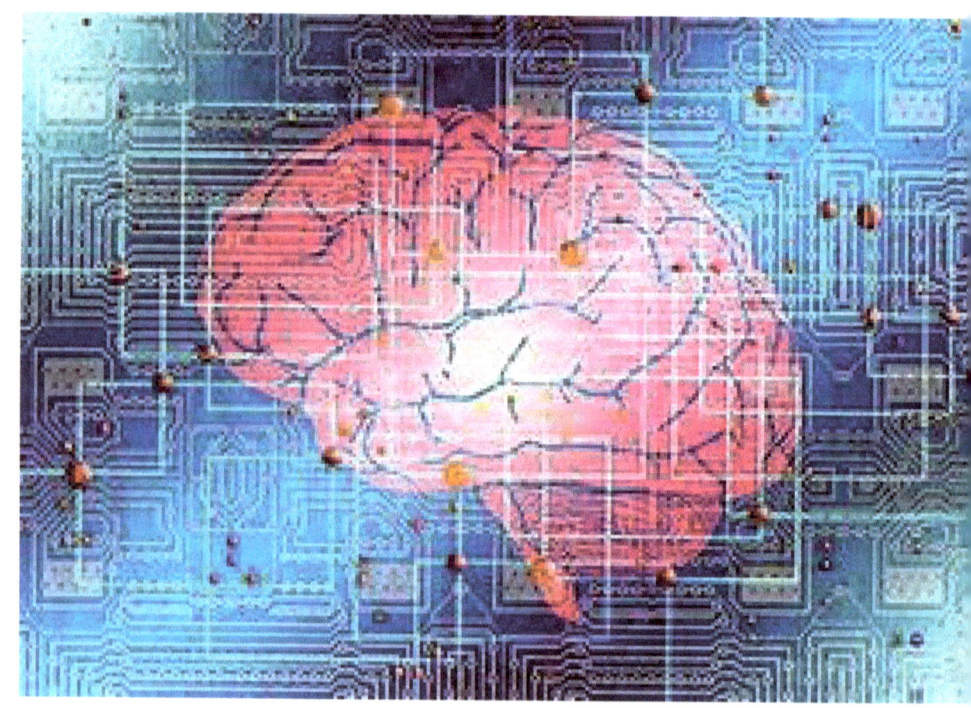

The human brain is equal parts radio and magnet—capable of broadcasting frequencies with astounding accuracy, and attracting anything imaginable through the mechanism of an unseen, yet very real, force.

# A Path Between the Sun and Moon

People now use virtual simulations to cop out of organic realities—to their physical, psychological, and spiritual detriment.

# A Path Between the Sun and Moon

The end of every
romantic
relationship marks
the death of a dream,
and birth of a new,
even greater, reality.

# A Path Between the Sun and Moon

For over seven years, I walked through a desert of continual pain and silence. Late in the journey, I discovered that I wasn't the desert, I wasn't the pain, and I wasn't the silence. I was the infinity beyond.

# A Path Between the Sun and Moon

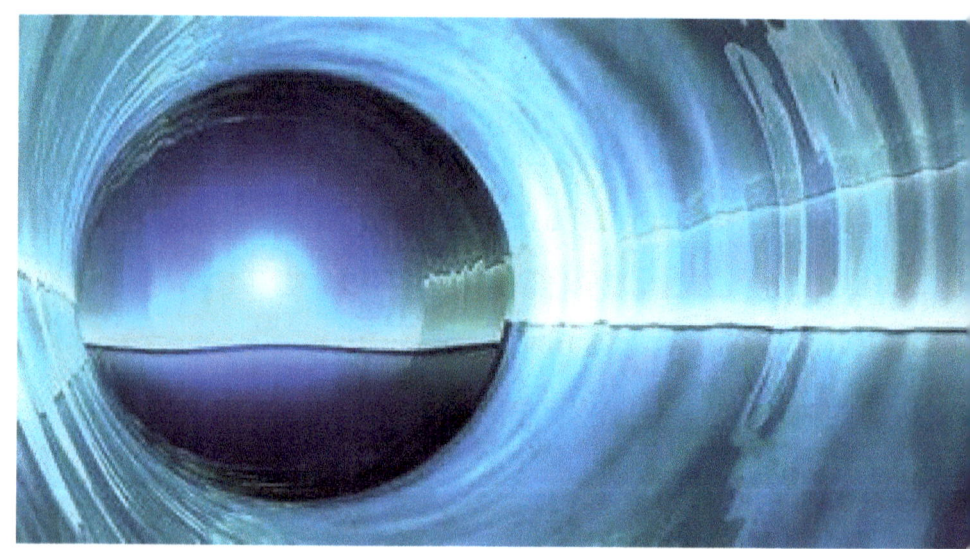

Life and death are
not diametrically
opposed finalities,
but mutually
dependent portals
into eternity.

We are not isolated
fragments in a
hostile universe; we
are intricately
woven threads in a
seamless tapestry.

# A Path Between the Sun and Moon

The perpetually guarded heart may never break, but it eventually suffocates from lack of love and genuine connection—a victim of its own invulnerability.

When your desire for the well-being of others exceeds your natural inclination toward self-preservation, your spirituality deepens immeasurably.

I frequently hear people say, "I just want some peace of mind!" But there is no peace of mind, only peace beyond mind—conscious respite from its vice-like grip—detached observation of its repetitive, highly conditioned chatter.

The more gifted and receptive the mind, the greater difficulty its occupant has finding freedom from the tyranny of unwanted thoughts.

Ours is a planet now overshadowed by the crystallized manifestations of fear.

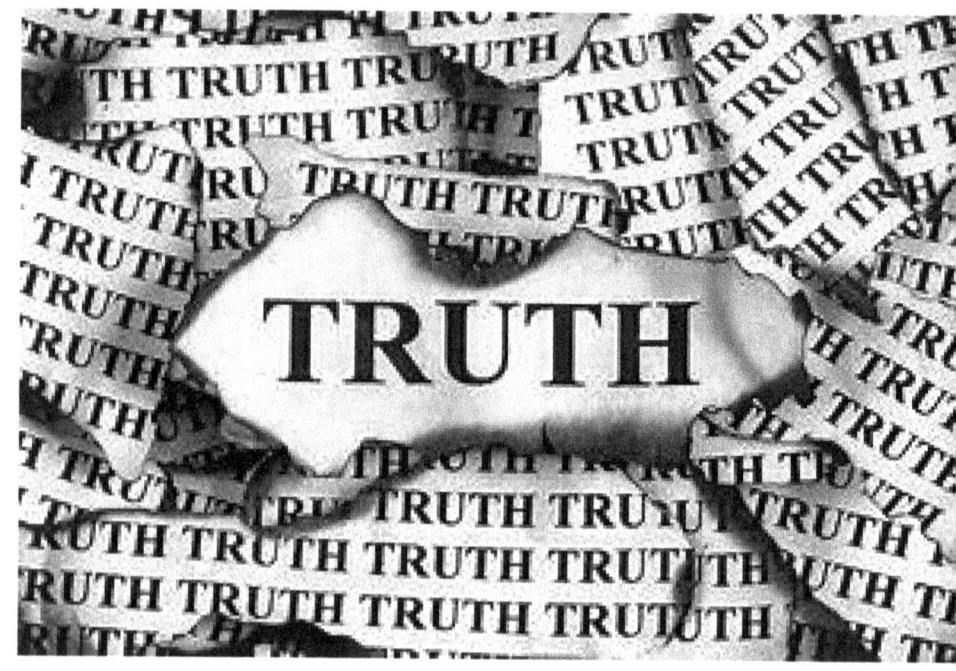

Whenever you bury
a lie, the truth is
eventually exhumed.

We simultaneously inhabit multiple dimensions—each a blooming flower in the garden of consciousness.

# A Path Between the Sun and Moon

# Spiritual truth, unlike illusion, has no expiration date.

Even the coal of unimaginable suffering can be transformed— shaped into a diamond of wisdom and compassion.

Everyone is destined
for greatness, but the
greatness they are
destined for may be
nothing like what
their ego hopes,
dreams, and imagines.

# A Path Between the Sun and Moon

The normalization
of insanity precedes
the fall of any
society.

# A Path Between the Sun and Moon

Seek rainbows in
thunderstorms and
new horizons
through the ash of
jettisoned dreams.

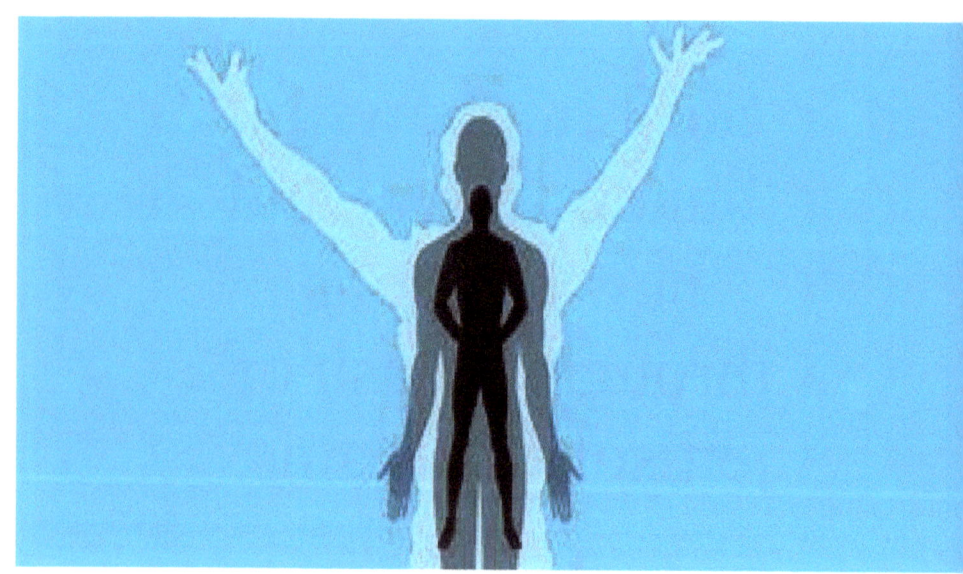

The only thing
sadder than physical
injury, illness,
disability, or death is
the belief that you
are only a body.

Judgment without discernment is self-indictment.

# A Path Between the Sun and Moon

Whatever you know
is nothing compared
to that which you
have yet to discover.

# A Path Between the Sun and Moon

In equanimity, there
is sanity; in
reactivity, madness.

If left unhealed,
internalized shadows
become externalized
nightmares.

# A Path Between the Sun and Moon

In nature, as in human experience, there is beauty and savagery, periods of lush abundance and utter desolation.

# A Path Between the Sun and Moon

Nature is the most incredibly synchronized clock ever conceived— and set to divinely orchestrated rhythm.

# A Path Between the Sun and Moon

For every truly knowledgeable, original, independent thinker, there are legions of ignorant minions eager to believe whatever lie they are told without so much as cursory investigation.

# A Path Between the Sun and Moon

Subjectivity and fear blur vision and warp perception quicker than a carnival hall-of-mirrors.

No character is without flaw; no life without tribulation.

# A Path Between the Sun and Moon

Peace is a quiet river; anger a howling, cyclonic wind that threatens to destroy whatever vessel dares cross its path.

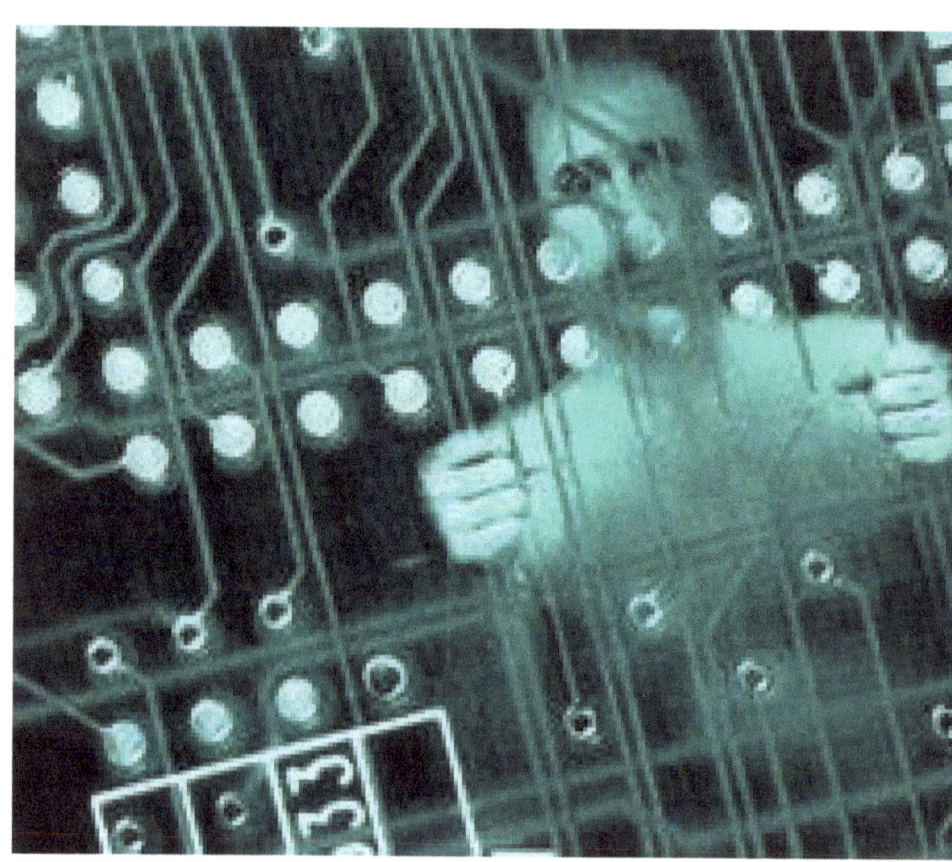

It's tragic to see people serving voluntary sentences in digital prisons, while the freedom and magic of real time/space pass them by.

# A Path Between the Sun and Moon

All religious, spiritual, and philosophical notions are merely way-showers— beacons of light against a backdrop of cosmic mystery.

# A Path Between the Sun and Moon

The ego is, by nature, limited to monochromatic vision in a technicolor universe.

Never expect
malignant intentions
to produce benign
results.

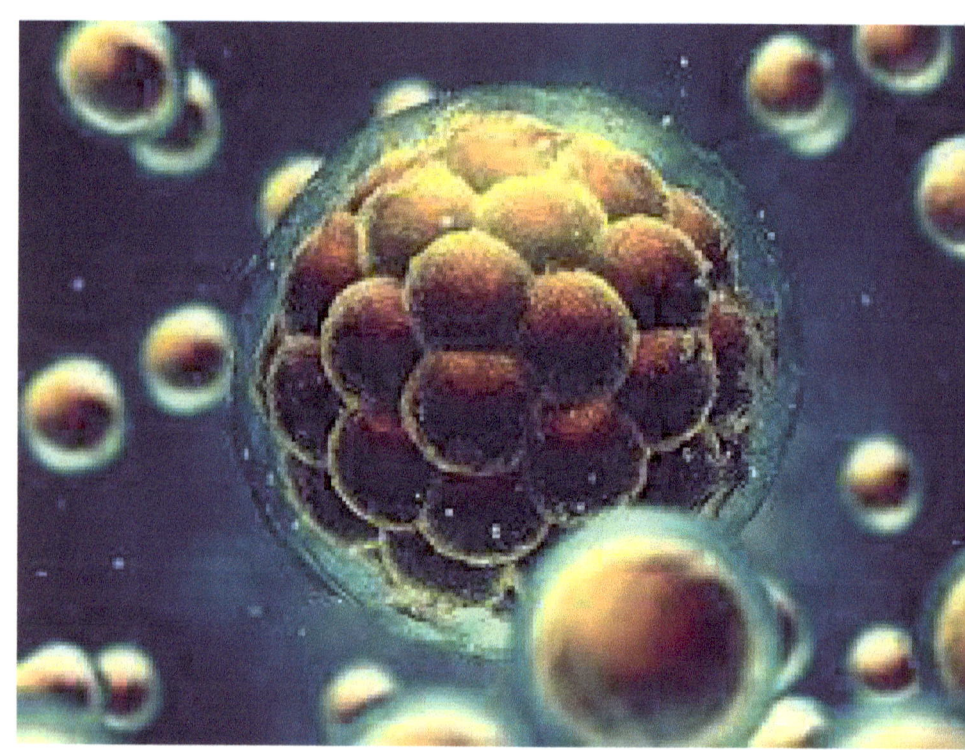

Before every visible expression of genius, there is an unseen genesis, and the embryonic stages of development that inevitably follow.

# A Path Between the Sun and Moon

Spiritual vision reveals that the easy, pleasure-filled path in life frequently leads nowhere…the difficult journey to beautiful, hard-won destinations.

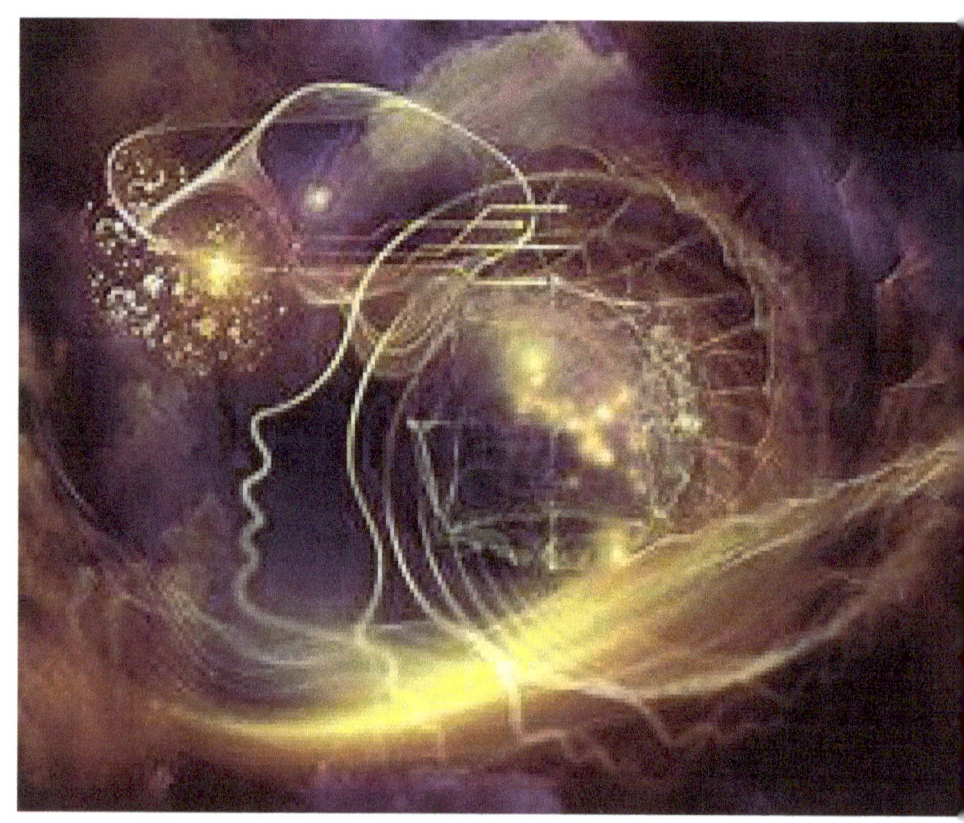

Always that which is imperceptible remains greater than that which can be detected through the five physical senses.

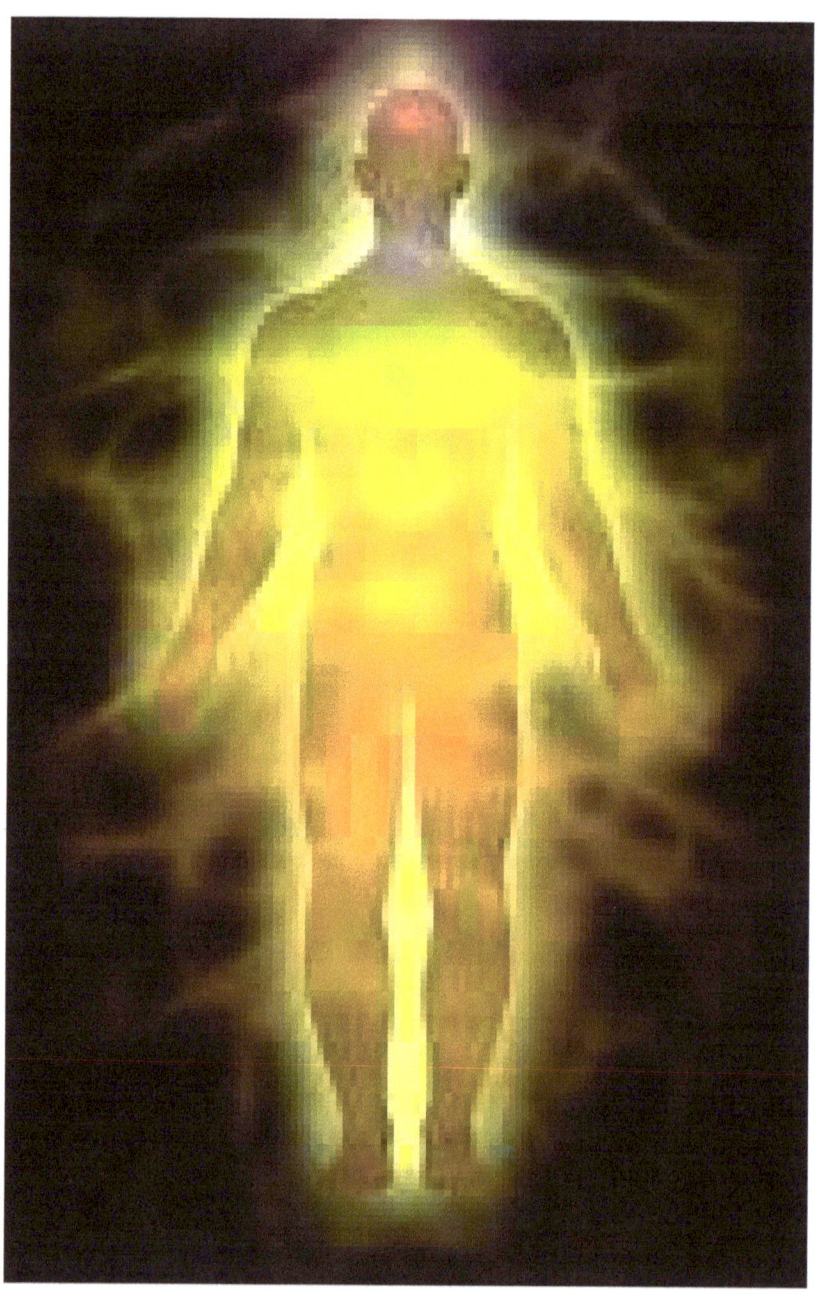

For some, it takes the death of the ego to spark the resurrection of the soul.

Most technology is
eventually rendered
obsolete—but never
the wisdom gleaned
from personal
experience.

# A Path Between the Sun and Moon

The fear of death
casts a long shadow;
the fear of life, even
longer…

Be humble enough
to understand the
difference between
what you really
believe and what
you truly know.

The story of every
life's journey ends
with a comma —
not a period.

One spiritually excavated, consciously realized truth is worth more than a thousand worldly pleasures.

It's better to be an honest failure than a disingenuous success.

What is commonly perceived as great misfortune in the world may amount to spiritual gain, and great fortune to spiritual loss.

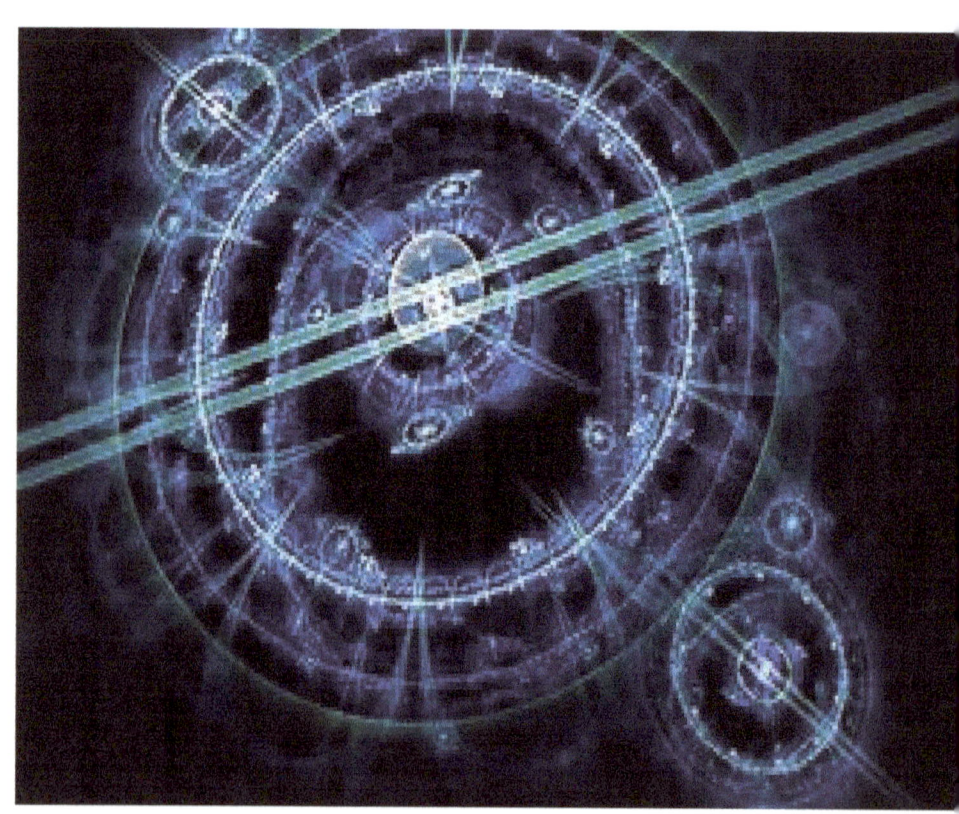

Few are they that
break free from the
shackles of time and
space before time
and space ultimately
force them to.

# A Path Between the Sun and Moon

Wisdom is a silent landscape that, once awakened, speaks in thunderous tones.

# A Path Between the Sun and Moon

Life is an infinite
expanse of
potentiality within
an indivisible
totality of existence.

Fear not that which
is humanly
disorienting, for it is
often spiritually
enlightening.

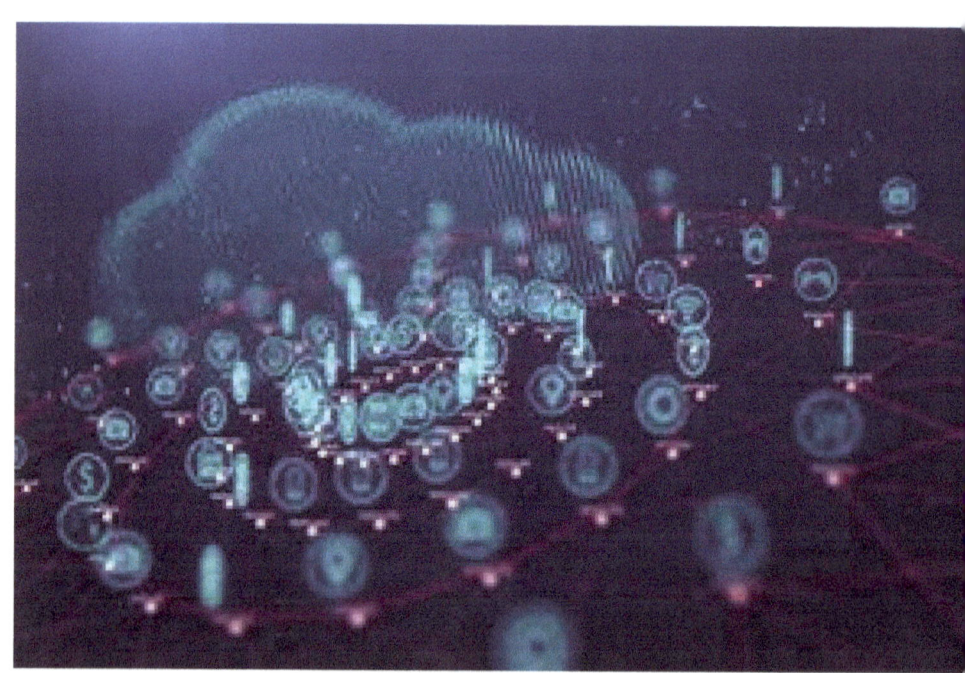

All "isms" and systems are, without exception, inherently flawed.

One can never
attract and sustain
greater love than
they are first willing
to give.

The moon doesn't speak to me, but still I hear her friendly whisper, through wind-tickled leaves, and tangled ribbons of light, bled out over slumbering waters.

# A Path Between the Sun and Moon

The light we seek
eludes us until the
darkness we avoid
becomes a trusted
friend.

What is
impenetrable to the
human intellect may
be suddenly
revealed in a
moment of spiritual
clarity.

# A Path Between the Sun and Moon

# A Path Between the Sun and Moon

# A Path Between the Sun and Moon

www.ingramcontent.com/pod-product-compliance
Lightning Source LLC
Chambersburg PA
CBHW041107280526
45792CB00010B/2329